IRELAND
Between the First and the Third Worlds

by

Carol Coulter

CAROL COULTER was born and spent her childhood in County Sligo, leaving to attend school in Dublin at the age of eleven. She studied English at Trinity College Dublin where she was active in student and left-wing politics. She has been a committed trade unionist and a socialist since then. In 1977 she started working as a freelance journalist and joined *The Irish Times* in 1986. She is interested in both Irish and world politics, and has visited Latin America and Eastern Europe in the course of her work.

First published in 1990 by
Attic Press,
44 East Essex Street,
Dublin 2.

British Library Cataloguing in Publication Data
Coulter, Carol
Ireland
1. Ireland. Politics
I. Title II. Series
320.9415

ISBN 0-946211-93-0

Acknowledgements

Thanks to John Daly, Declan Kiberd and Harry Vince for their comments and suggestions.

Cover Design: Paula Nolan
Typesetting: Attic Press
Printing: Elo Press

IRELAND

Between the First and the Third Worlds

There has been much debate recently about the use of the female image to represent Ireland, ranging from the academic discourse of the Yeats Summer School to the polemical - and banned - film by the Derry Film Video Group, *Mother Ireland*. This could be dismissed as self-indulgence on the part of literary critics or radicals' nostalgia for the language of revolutionary nationalism, were it not for the resurgence of this image in new guise in contemporary political debate. Our political leaders and commentators of today are every bit as ready as our poets and revolutionaries to turn to the language of personal relationships when seeking to express and explain national aspirations. However, the terminology is different.

This is particularly evident in the sphere of Anglo-Irish relations, which are frequently spoken of in language normally applied to the field of marital breakdown. Ronan Fanning writes of 'the bond with Britain', while 'the totality of relationships between these two islands' has come to be a catch-phrase. Speaking of the Anglo-Irish agreement, James Molyneaux described it as 'two nations locked in a loveless marriage which has irretrievably broken down', ironically echoing Seamus Heaney's poem, *Act of Union*. Equally common are exhortations to forget the past, to forge a new relationship based on new realities and mutual respect, to embrace 'forgiveness' and 'reconciliation.'

All this conjures up an image of a marriage gone wrong, of years of bitterness and discord, certainly, leaving a heritage of suspicion and querulousness. But wiser counsel demands that all this is put behind us and that a new relationship is forged on the basis of mutual, if more limited, cooperation - for the sake of the children.

Fundamental to the concept of marriage is that it is a relationship freely entered into by both parties. If it goes wrong there are faults on both sides and there is no point in recriminations or in apportioning blame. All sensible people agree that the separation should be effected with the minimum of confrontation.

However, if we pursue the image of male-female relations with reference to the history of those between Britain and Ireland, a more appropriate image is that of kidnap and multiple rape - the enforced domination of a nation and centuries of exploitation. This suggests a different trajectory for the relationship which follows the escape of the victim who should not be expected to behave like an estranged spouse.

This use of language is more than a question of style. It is part of the development of a modern political ideology in this country which seeks to minimise our colonial history and heritage, and therefore ignore the implications of this history for an analysis of our present problems and solutions for the future. If we come to believe in a past unsullied by colonial conquest we can look forward to a future in which we are no less - and no more - than any other Western European nation, entering into a new experience of Europe on the same basis as everyone else.

In this pamphlet I want to argue that any discussion of Irish politics must start from our experience of colonialism and imperialism, which ended in a compromise with the former coloniser which denied true emancipation. This has left us with a heritage which included political institutions designed to prevent significant social change, and it is futile for feminists, socialists, or anyone seeking it to do so through them. To help us understand this, we should look to the experiences of other former colonies and also to our fellow-Europeans in East and Central Europe which also experienced national oppression.

The Irish 'national question' is thus as much at the centre of seeking a solution to the social, economic and political ills of the south as to ending the political crisis in the north. I argue for a reappraisal of the radical and revolutionary content of Irish nationalism, freed from the pseudo-nationalist ideology created by the architects of the southern state, and fused with the new radical thinking now emanating from these other former colonies and subjugated nations.

It is of course undeniable that we are part of Europe, geographically, historically and ethnically. We can neither deny it nor imagine a future outside it. But this must be refracted through our fundamental historical experience, which has formed our political institutions and our consciousness, with all its contradictions and complexities. And that is a colonial experience. Therefore the analogues of our institutions, our culture and our political life and expectations are to be found more in other former colonies than in the old imperialist power of Western Europe. The countries of Central Europe, most of them formerly part of the Austro-Hungarian empire, are another matter.

The suggestion that Ireland should be compared to Third World countries is often met with a combination of derision and indignation. What! Are we not white? And European? And, compared with the countries of the Third World, wealthy? And educated?

These objections are all true, but none of them negate our history and the political heritage it has left us, which has profound implications for the permanence and stability of our institutions and their capacity to permit major reform.

Indeed, we are not alone among former colonies in seeking to deny a family relationship with the lower-class members of this club, those with teeming masses of black or brown uneducated poor, the deserving recipients of our charity and our prayers.

Argentina is a case in point. Like the Irish, the Argentinians are white, well-educated, European in culture and outlook and, until recently, relatively wealthy. Indeed, they were the biggest consumers of meat in the world in the 1950s and 1960s, with a high consumption of bread, rice, fresh fruit and other components of a balanced diet. Primary education was free and compulsory, and the state also provided free or almost free public secondary and technical schools - somewhat like the situation in Ireland until the end of the 1960s.

Not surprisingly, Argentinians reacted angrily to any attempt to include them in the Third World. However, their political history undermined their claim to be a fully paid-up member of the First. They had an embarrassing tendency towards military coups. And events of the last twelve months show the fragility of their economic prosperity, based as it was on an economy which developed in total dependence on imperialism, particularly British and North American imperialism.

Interestingly, the Argentinian poet Luis Borges recognised the positive aspects of this experience both for his country and for Ireland:

> Our tradition is all of Western culture ... Veblen says that the Jews are outstanding in Western culture because they act within that culture and, at the same time, do not feel tied to it by any special devotion ... and we can say the same of the Irish in English culture ... I believe that we Argentines, we South Americans in general, are in an analogous situation; we can handle all European themes, handle them without superstition, with an irreverence which can have, and already does have, fortunate consequences.

I would suggest that it is not either geographical location or level of economic development which explains our institutions and allows us to plan for the future in a realistic way. Rather it is our historically-defined place in international relations and the political institutions we have inherited from the past, themselves the accumulation of battles fought between different social forces.

IRISH NATIONALISM - A MANY-STRANDED TRADITION

The Palestinian writer and critic, Edward Said, has pointed out that there are two distinct political moments during a nationalist revival, the first the assertion of the reality of imperialist domination and the need to escape from it, the second the development of the 'post-nationalist' theme of liberation implicit in the works of Connolly, Garvey, Marti, Mariategi and DuBois.

The struggle for Irish independence has, since the latter part of the nineteenth century, been fused with the struggle for the social emancipation of the most oppressed sections of the Irish population, the tenant farmers and workers. These two strands cohabited in an uneasy alliance and the future of the poor was often sacrificed for the sake of the political aspirations of the nascent Irish middle class.

This was not just an Irish problem. The labour movement which developed in Europe and America in the nineteenth century, and expanded throughout the world in the twentieth century, never saw its own, independent role within the nationalist movement. During the crucial period in Irish history, the Second International, dominated by parties from the major imperialisms of Europe, could offer nothing to tenant farmers and workers in Ireland or anywhere else struggling against colonial exploitation and facing the half-heartedness of their own bourgeoisie.

Women's organisations emerged also at this time, and generally sided with the most oppressed foot-soldiers of the struggle against British imperialism and its local allies. In her thorough study of women and Irish nationalism, *Unmanageable Revolutionaries*, Margaret Ward points out that the women of the Ladies Land League were far more radical than Parnell in pursuing the demands of the tenants; that Inghinidhe na hEireann, unlike Sinn Féin, campaigned to support the workers during the 1913 Lockout and the women in Cumann na mBan were among the most radical opponents of the Treaty.

The development of these nationalist women's organisations coincided with that of the suffragette movement and, indeed, there was frequent cooperation between these two strands of the women's movement. This period of national awakening, therefore, saw the emergence of a plethora of groups, movements and organisations operating in the social, political and cultural arenas. Whatever their common national aspirations, they often represented different interests and as the national struggle unfolded some would come to dominate over others.

Modern critics of Irish nationalism represent it as monolithic, a unified ideology which produced as its inevitable embodiment the southern Irish state. This ideology is seen as socially and economically conservative, Gaelic, deeply imbued with catholicism, narrow and inward-looking. The state it would produce would inevitably contain these flaws, it is argued.

This is a kind of retrospective argument. Faced with the modern Irish state it is easy to find in Irish nationalism all the elements which serve as its ideology. (By this I mean the southern state. Only in the southern part of the partitioned country has there been the development of any state. The northern part cannot really be called a state in its own right but is rather an extension of the British state, distinguished from it only by its specially repressive characteristics in the field of personal and civil rights.)

The many other elements which were undoubtedly present in Irish nationalism - not just at the level of ideology, but expressed in living people - ranging from socialism and feminism to religious scepticism and various forms of mysticism, were defeated and their adherents marginalised or forced to keep their dissident views to themselves. This defeat was by no means inevitable. Nor is it irreversible.

The historical point when this occurred was with the Treaty, although there were several other important moments around that, from the formation of the First Dáil, through the Civil War and culminating in the 1937 Constitution, which followed Fianna Fáil's entry into the Dáil and subsequent election victory. This period was marked by social unrest, by strikes, factory and land occupations, in parts of the north as well as the south, involving protestants in the north as well as the predominantly catholic workers of the south.

No-one should be surprised at this. The decade from the Rising to the British General Strike of 1926 was one of revolutionary activity throughout Europe, with millions of women and men seeking fundamental changes in their circumstances.

The Irish state which came into being in this period was, in Said's words, 'The old colonial structures replicated in new national terms'. In this it can be compared with many other states which were formed following the formal ending of imperialist domination, but without a radical transfer of power between social classes. Indeed, the maintenance of 'old colonial structures' was imperative precisely in order to prevent a transfer of political power to those who bore the brunt of imperialist exploitation. The new ruling class had no structure of its own to put in their place and politics, like nature, abhors a vacuum.

DISGUISING THE OLD

Central to the functioning of the new Irish state was the civil service. This was maintained intact, with the civil servants, including very senior ones, changing masters with equanimity. In his autobiography, *Man of No Property* (Volume Two), Todd Andrews describes the mistrust with which Fianna Fáil viewed the civil service when it came to power. But it did nothing to dismantle it, or even to purge it, thus revealing its eagerness to model the new Irish state on the old colonial one.

This was carried through to the form of the parliamentary system, with its upper and lower houses, and the maintenance of the legal system, even including the absurdity of keeping 'republican' judges and barristers in wigs and gowns. The laws adopted earlier in England to meet the needs of colonialism and finance capital were kept intact on the statute books, and to this day legal precedent set in Britain is used in Irish courts.

Another institution which survived the transition from British to Irish rule was the catholic church. Indeed, it did so with its power enhanced. The special kind of collaboration between the Church and the State which is such a mark of the modern Irish state began under the British administration and was developed when independence was established. Without the roots it had put down in the education and health systems under British rule, it could not play the role in them it does today.

The institutions inherited from Britain reflect the specific character of former British colonies, as opposed to former colonies of other powers, particularly Spain and Portugal. Although, like them, it ruled by military domination, applied when the need arose, its grip was maintained through its administration, and this system survived its departure.

British domination characteristically took the form of a unique combination of a civil service modelled on its own and cooperation with native power structures. India had a ready-made and long-established social structure with which the British system was able to combine. In the case of Ireland, however, Britain's attempt to incorporate the native Irish ruling caste failed very early on. Later it tried to use the Church, and it is interesting to see how Britain cultivated the catholic church throughout the nineteenth century, as it became clear that resistance to its rule was becoming more and more widespread.

Spain, despite its extensive colonial possessions, was unable (because of the backwardness of its own society, dominated by an inert and profligate aristocracy) to develop a real colonial administration. It exported to its colonies a habit of seizing and holding vast tracts of land and of raising pillaging armies dominated by this land-owning class. Most Latin American countries continue to be dominated by a small class of big land-owners, who provided the basis for the development of much of the rest of native capital, and most of them also have huge armies, frequently the only permanent institution in the country apart from the catholic church.

So the countries of Latin American, including those, like Argentina and Brazil, which have controlled great wealth, look very different from Ireland. They are dominated by land-based oligarchies. They have vast armies with a sense of political mission, even if not always fulfilled. We have a tiny army, not linked to any political party or ruling group, which has no will - or capacity - to play a political role.

But this should not lead us to conclude that the Latin American countries are part of post-colonial society and we are not, that they are thus characterised as of the 'Third World' while we are conspicuously of the 'First'. It means only that the colonial structures we have inherited are different. Different, but equally inherited. It could also be pointed out that India, like us a former British colony, has a vast civil and public service and an army which has never played a part in politics.

Societies and states which struggle to find a space between their own history as colonies and the domination of the world by the big imperialist powers, while seeking simultaneously to preserve their social order undisturbed, carry the marks of this on their political institutions and their culture. These marks are different from those borne by the major European countries, including the smaller ones like Holland and Belgium, whose political development, by and large, follows their economic development and needs.

Irish political institutions, political culture, language and habits, have, I would argue, more in common with many Latin American and indeed Eastern European countries than with our Western European neighbours. Poland, Hungary and Czechoslovakia also spent centuries under the domination of a powerful neighbour (or two, in the case of poor Poland). They too suffered from the suppression of their language, culture and, in the case of Poland and Czechoslovakia, of their religion. They also experienced the growth of large nationalist movements in the nineteenth century in which literature and culture played a major role. They won their independence in the revolutionary surge sparked off by the First World War.

Since the end of the Second World War the history of these countries has been very different from ours. But that is a period of only forty-five years, far from enough to create a new political culture. Further, their subsequent experience of foreign domination and, in the cases of Hungary or Czechoslovakia, of invasion, have strong echoes of the past, even if their source, and the social system they accompany, is different.

The search for a definition of identity and real sovereignty, the intensity of cultural debate and its fusion with political discussion, albeit linked to the political problem of the fight against totalitarianism, have interesting parallels with the contemporary Irish experience. An attempt to find a 'European identity' on the basis of parallels with France, Holland or even Portugal has far less basis in historical reality.

Turning again to the parallels with Latin America, we find that, like them, our major political parties have their origins in a revolutionary nationalist movement, still reflected, however shamefacedly, in their constitutions and rhetoric. Even Fine Gael pays ritual obeisance to the aim of the establishment of a united and independent Ireland, though the party which has appropriated this objective as its own is Fianna Fáil.

LEGITIMISING THE NEW STATE

However, unlike the countries of Latin America, Irish independence was not established unequivocally, and it took some years for the new state to gain acceptance among the whole population. Fianna Fáil and the catholic church were both crucial to this.

The Church only accepted Fianna Fáil when it indicated its willingness to accept the legitimacy of the Free State, by its decision to take seats in a newly-created twenty-six county parliament. The Church's first commitment was to the Free State, whose foundation it supported to the hilt, justifying the draconian measures taken by the Cumann na nGaedheal government to consolidate it.

Thus began the relationship of mutual dependence between the new Irish state and the catholic church. From the outset they supported each other and during the early years of the state, the Church established its grip on key parts of the public service, notably education and health, and had its moral and social teaching enshrined in legislation.

In fact, the control the Church exercises on health and education is much more than a moral one. It provides a material base (in terms of property like the valuable site of Carysfort College, now for sale) for the exercise of political power and influence in a broader sphere.

In the beginning, the custodians for the new Irish state were Cumann na nGaedheal, a party of heterogeneous origins. Although born of a split in Sinn Féin, it quickly attracted the remnants of the formerly anti-Sinn Féin forces. Its ideology was defined rather by what it opposed (republicanism, subversion and chaos) than by what it stood for and, although cowed by the catholic church, it did not have the self-confidence to establish the intimate relationship with it that de Valera's Fianna Fáil did.

But this came only with de Valera's conversion to constitutional politics. In *The Rise and Decline of Fianna Fáil* Kevin Boland describes how this came about: 'There was no acceptance of the legitimacy of the Free State, which had been officially characterised at the La Scala [meeting] as a "pretence at democracy". It was merely a question of recognising the *de facto* situation for practical reasons.' He points out that what made the southern state 'legitimate' for Fianna Fáil and their supporters was the adoption of the 1937 (Fianna Fáil) Constitution. From this time on, he writes, 'there could be no doubt, in the mind of any reasonable person, of the legitimacy of the elected government'. It was the election of Fianna Fáil to government, and the subsequent elaboration of a constitution, which rendered the state legitimate in the eyes of the mass of the people, he claims.

There is more than an element of truth in this assertion. Before the decision of de Valera to enter the Dáil, both the Dáil itself and the Cumann na nGaedheal government were viewed with suspicion and hostility by a large proportion of the population, and this party's early rule was accompanied by severe repression of and discrimination against suspected republican sympathisers. Nor was it any better for others who hoped to see liberation after the departure of the British. The rights and conditions of women, workers and the poor generally were pushed into the background or ignored, and a series of laws passed (on divorce, censorship and the like) reflecting the growing hold of the catholic church on public life to the detriment of women and the poor. The new government singularly failed to establish popular support.

This was evident in the first post-Treaty election, where the governing party received only 39% of the vote, despite the fact that most of the active opposition was on the run or interned and that the resources of the state it controlled were used to disrupt the Sinn Féin campaign. The latter, in these very adverse conditions, received 26.7%. Given that this was on the basis of the non-recognition of the state, it was hardly a recipe for political stability.

So the acceptance by Fianna Fáil of the legitimacy of the state in the south was absolutely crucial for establishing its stability. Although people were war-weary and demoralised, and those who sought radical change had been defeated, without the foundation and construction of Fianna Fáil as a bridge between a large dissident minority and the new state, it would have remained as something alien to a large proportion of the population. It would have required constant coercion to ensure political quietude, with the attendant danger of an explosion of discontent - a situation not dissimilar to that which prevailed in the north.

A new past and a new character were created for Mother Ireland, de Valera's metaphorical bride, by Fianna Fáil. If Ireland was a woman, she was also Irish-speaking, catholic and (paradoxically) a virgin. If she had once been kidnapped and raped, no offspring ensued and thus no provision needed to be made for them and it could all be put behind her and a new, pure life built. History was rewritten to present successive nationalist movements as expressions of an uninterrupted fight for the catholic faith. Nationality was presented as identical with religion, thus removing any necessity to look closely at the real social, political and cultural content of colonial domination. Doing so might prompt people to make comparisons uncomfortable to the new rulers.

The ideology created in these years, with the enthusiastic support and participation of the catholic church, justified the growing grip of Fianna Fáil on the machinery of the state, and on the development of an infrastructure for the fledgling independent economy.

Control of the state also meant control of patronage, and this control was used by both major parties to advance the interests of their supporters. At a national level it meant that supporters had access to jobs in the judiciary and at the head of state-sponsored bodies. Later it might mean a state grant. At local level, which was more important in terms of popular support, a word from a TD could mean a job working with the county council or one of the state companies - the main sources of employment outside agriculture in the 1940s, '50s and early '60s. It was understood that in return, the recipients of the favour, their family and friends, would vote for the obliging TD, and this understanding was usually faithfully honoured. Thus were people bound both to the state and the party.

As Frank McDonald of *The Irish Times* has pointed out, it was a logical step from this to more direct corruption, the exchange of money for favours, which surfaced in the recent Dublin planning scandal. The culture of corruption, a feature of all neo-colonial societies, had already been created, albeit within the framework of legality up to then.

It is true that in other Western European countries - and in the United States of America - senior public appointments often depend on party affiliation. But this is not true at a general level and even where local government officials control access to certain jobs, this has operated in a context where people could find employment elsewhere in the economy. It did not act as political cement, binding people to one or other political party, in the way it did in Ireland.

THE LATIN AMERICAN EXPERIENCE

One must look to countries outside Western Europe and the United States of America to find analogues for the way in which the major political parties, particularly Fianna Fáil, operate. While in Colombia, early in 1989, I was surprised to discover how familiar the political scene was. Political life was dominated by two political parties whose history was marked by intermittent war between them, but who had come to a truce on the basis of an agreement that neither of them would seek to monopolise political power and patronage. Both are linked to the big land-owners, big business - and individuals within both parties have links with the drug mafia.

The political system was, and remains, one in which access to any area of public life, to even the most menial job in the public service, is controlled by the major political parties. This has been modified in recent years, but until recently the tendrils of the political parties, especially the Liberal party, reached into trade unions, municipal organisations and the limited public service, binding people to the state far more effectively than any intermittent participation in the electoral process. Serious political questions are not decided in elections, where there is no real choice, and the rigid political and military structures, based on the need to keep the mass of the population out of active political life, will permit of no fundamental change.

Our institutions share this inflexibility. Unlike the political institutions of our Western European neighbours, which evolved out of the changing needs of the indigenous ruling groups, they were born of a compromise between the former colonising power and the native ruling class to whom they were handing over. Essential to that compromise was the maintenance of continuity with the old regime, while giving the appearance of creating a new one, ostensibly the product of years of popular struggle. Hence the green post-boxes, the *cúpla focal*, the Irish names for parliamentary institutions and parties ... But behind the green and gaelic facade lie the heritage of British legislation, of a two-tier parliament, of a civil service and police modelled on the lines of the colonial power, all upholding a social system entirely in accord with the interests of that power.

For some years now political commentators and politicians from Fine Gael and the pre-Damascus road Progressive Democrats have been bewailing the 'clientelism' of Irish politics. People see their TDs as the donors of favours, as their mediators, and the politicians are therefore forced to spend their time dealing with petty individual problems rather than concerning themselves with affairs of state. Casting longing glances at Britain and continental Europe, these politicians deplore the blinkered ignorance of the Irish electorate which fails to recognise the lofty tasks to which politicians aspire, and expects them to be errand boys and girls instead.

In September last Padraig Flynn, Minister for the Environment and archetypal Fianna Fáil politician (rural-based, catholic, conservative), made a spirited defense of clientelism in the pages of *The Irish Times* where he argued that people feel alienated from and fearful of 'bureaucracy'. They feel the need for a more approachable figure to explain its workings and mediate between them and the faceless bureaucrats, to find individual details which might modify uncaring decisions. In his second article he quoted a survey of clientelism which found that rural-based people and the working class were more likely to believe in the efficacy of this kind of political brokerage than those from urban and middle-class backgrounds - significantly, precisely the traditional base of Fianna Fáil.

These are also the people who withheld initial recognition from the state, and who were lured into becoming involved in the political process through this mediating service on behalf of Fianna Fáil. Padraig Flynn rightly fears the danger of removing this conduit between the state and those he describes as suffering from 'isolation, alienation and a sense that you don't matter'. It is the function of politicians, he argued, to lessen people's sense of alienation from the state and political institutions they mistrust.

The foundation of Fianna Fáil and the manner in which it proceeded to organise and involve people in the complex political process, including elements of patronage, clientelism and corporatism, all 'part of what we are', was intended to legitimise the state and make it stable. However, in so doing Fianna Fáil made that state peculiarly unable to accommodate major change. It depends on a fragile balance between different interest groups, whose interests were built into its foundations, and which cannot now be disturbed.

Most conspicuous among them is the catholic church whose ownership (literally) of large areas of public life, like education and health, was a cornerstone of the state and sanctioned in the Constitution. Changes have been made, not by the election of a party dedicated to developing and implementing a programme of change, as happens elsewhere in Western Europe, but by negotiation between the government of the day and different interest groups. Which party is in power is largely immaterial, though Fianna Fáil has cultivated a wider variety of interest groups. Questions like social welfare, wages policy, health and education policy have been worked out more in the framework of discussions between the government, employers and unions than through any party implementing a political programme.

THE POSITIVE SIDE OF POLITICAL DISILLUSIONMENT

Yet all this has not succeeded in removing the vague contempt, the suspicion of impermanence, from the state, its laws and institutions. The lack of respect for the law gives rise to much public hand-wringing, and there is no doubt that the level of defiance of traffic and parking legislation, for example, is far higher here than in Britain. However defiance goes beyond parking on double yellow lines or cycling without a light on your bike. In September 1989 hundreds of people in Waterford kidnapped council workers sent to cut off water for non-payment of water rates.

The 1983 amendment to the Constitution provides another example. Although the Society for the Protection of Unborn Children (SPUC) obtained an injunction to prevent the dissemination of abortion information, this was recently defied by several student unions whose leaders indicated their willingness to go to jail in defiance of the law. SPUC suggested that the issue then was one of application of the law, and was no longer one of abortion. But this found few echoes from politicians, who knew full well that in this country the enactment of a law by parliament - or by referendum - does not mean it will be obeyed. Endorsement by political institutions alone does not guarantee acceptance. The law must reflect a consensus negotiated outside parliament.

Why should people vote for parties offering them a programme for radical change? Understanding how the system works, they know that this would not happen, that things would go on much as before, with the influence of the powerful interest groups holding sway. So why not vote for a negotiator, a mediator, someone you can badger and blackmail into representing your individual interests?

This gives rise to despair among those politicians, especially on the left, who seek change through the Irish political system. But it has a positive side as well. The relative unimportance of the Dáil in the decision-making process means, not only that forces like industrialists, farmers and lay catholic organisations can effect change through pressure, but so can other extra-parliamentary groups if they can win support.

A small example is the Rape Crisis Centre, which started off with a handful of women and no resources, but through some sympathy in the media and considerable organisational ability on the part of its organisers achieved changes in the treatment of rape victims by the police and the courts, achieved some state support for its services and influenced the report of the Law Reform Commission on rape, all in a relatively short time. In Britain much bigger pressure groups on various issues have been running around in circles for ages without making the slightest impact on Margaret Thatcher's government, for whom there is only one reality - her majority in parliament. In contrast, many of the changes in social legislation in Ireland have come about as a result of pressure from organised lobbies applied to whatever government was in power. This could be a very positive mechanism for people, especially women, who have little weight in the political system and political parties.

The fact that elections change very little in Ireland implies actual or potential disillusionment with the political system. As I have argued above, Fianna Fáil sought, and succeeded, in acting as a buffer between potentially disillusioned voters and that system. But now that is threatened by the crisis in Fianna Fáil induced by the changes within it, culminating in the leadership's acceptance of coalition.

This should be a cause of rejoicing, not dismay, among those who seek radical change in Ireland, north and south. The political system in this part of the country is not amenable to fundamental change, any more than it is in the north. A crisis in its institutions should prompt all those anxious to see change to reconsider its foundation, the premises on which it is based, its ideology, and to look beyond them to a new framework for the whole island.

Thus, far from the 'national question' being a device to divert the attention of people in the south from their immediate and day-to-day problems, it is intimately connected to the solution of these problems.

The 'national question' concerns the capacity of the people living in the south to live a life free of exploitation and oppression as much as it concerns the need to end the decades of discrimination, repression and warfare in the north, and all that derive from them.

An uneasy, unarticulated suspicion that this might indeed be so has given rise to a fear of nationalism among the southern middle class, expressed in the concern that the 'trouble' in the north will 'spill over' into the south, seeping into our carefully stabilised society like a malign virus.

Of course for the unemployed youth of Darndale and Tallaght there is little hope except that the instability in the north will indeed 'spill over' and threaten the system that has so alienated them, and so among the working class and especially the youth there is considerable, if unformed and inarticulate, support for the Irish Republican Army (IRA). But the uncomfortable recognition of this only serves to reinforce the dominant consensus that the 'trouble' in the north must be contained at all costs, and the IRA, now cast as the source of it all, destroyed.

THE CREATION OF AN IDEOLOGY

The past twenty years have seen the growth of a consensus among politicians and commentators that the northern problem must be contained and, it is hastily added, of course ultimately solved. The first priority, therefore, is to contain and if possible reduce the violence.

Here common cause has been made with Britain, and hence the apologetic down-grading of the history of colonisation, the substitution of language describing colonisers' rapaciousness with that of marital discord. Hence also the embarrassed disavowal of 'old fashioned nationalism', the fear that this will jeopardise the prospects of a new harmony with our estranged neighbours and of 'reconciliation' between the 'two traditions' in the north, and ultimately on this island, necessary to 'peaceful reunification.'

In fact, this developing new orthodoxy is part of a continuum with the 'old nationalism' it seeks to repudiate. The real break in the political thinking in the southern state came, not with the reputed 'revisionism', but with the Treaty, Partition and the need for an ideology to legitimate them. For all its bluster, the nationalism used to justify the formation and consolidation of the new state was in fact a carefully constructed bulwark against a resurgence of a radical anti-imperialism that, drawing on the grievances of the artificially-created minority of the north, might fuse with the disappointment of the small farmers, women, workers and also intellectuals in the south who found their circumstances little changed - or changed for the worse - by independence.

Yet for the 'traditional' nationalist ideology to be developed in the 1920s, '30s and '40s, it needed to contain elements of the real experience of the mass of the Irish people, the experience of dispossession, oppression and discrimination which fed the successive nationalist movements of the nineteenth century. The native language and culture really were suppressed, hundreds of thousands of people really were dispossessed of their land and displaced, over a million really did starve during the Famine ... and these and other experiences really were the result of British policy at the time. The existence of anti-imperialist sentiment (not surprisingly, predominantly anti-British in form) among Irish people is due, not to a bigoted education, but to this reality.

What the Free State and its ideologists sought to do was take the revolutionary sting out of it, rewrite and oversimplify this experience and represent it as centuries-long struggle for formal independence and for the untrammelled flowering of a catholic identity, after years of subjugation to the protestant identity of the conqueror. A catholic state for a catholic people indeed. Further, 'patriotism' now became identified with the economic and political consolidation of this state, under the leadership of the 'entrepreneurial class' as described by Kevin Boland when he outlined the early ideology of Fianna Fáil.

It suited this class down to the ground to entrust the education of the youth, and the formulation of social policy, to the catholic church. The outlook which it put forward in the 1930s, with its corporate view of society, sought to deny class divisions, to preach satisfaction with the economic status quo and to keep women and youth subordinated to husbands and fathers. The asceticism it preached conformed perfectly to de Valera's vision of rural-based frugal simplicity with the illusory national independence presented as a consolation for the lack of material comforts.

Consciously or not, the nationalist ideology developed at this time was deeply partitionist in nature. Presenting the southern state as the achievement of the fight for national freedom was in fundamental contradiction to a perspective of the freedom and independence of the whole country. It destroyed any common heritage with the protestant small farmers and working class of the country, most of them living in the northern part of it. It provided unionist politicians with ample ammunition to bolster their contention that Irish independence meant Rome rule and economic backwardness. Unionist ideology among the protestant working class, weakened during the revolutionary upheavals of the 1913-1923 decade when it appeared life was about to change fundamentally for everyone, was reinforced so that it is stronger now than ever before.

It was a short step from this for the ideologists of the south to present protestants and protestantism (whatever that may be) as the antithesis of Irish nationalism, as foreign in every sense, even, in moments of intense rhetoric, as representing the historical enemy. Meanwhile, with typical hypocrisy, they were slipping privileges to the small number of protestants who lived in the south in the form of highly subsidised schools and hospitals, and encouraging the continued advance of those among them who held economic power. Thus was bought their silence concerning the suppression of personal liberties promoted by the catholic church, and its control over vast areas of public life. The protestant churches were well-versed in rendering unto Caesar the things that were Caesar's; they had been doing so in Ireland for far longer than their catholic counterparts. In the north, meanwhile, they enjoyed unrestricted influence in government, with clerics often participating openly in the Orange Order and the Unionist party.

This division of labour in helping to govern the whole country worked perfectly until the 1960s. The necessity of opening up the Irish economy had by then eroded the old kind of nationalism and its rural, catholic values. But its crisis came with the outbreak of open rebellion in the north.

So now it is succeeded by talk of the necessity of 'reconciling' the 'two traditions', retrospectively legitimising partition by representing it as the inevitable outcome of the presence on this island of two distinct ethnic, cultural and political entities. No-one stops to ask - what two traditions? It is assumed that they refer to realities behind the rural, Gaelic, catholic ideology of Irish nationalism and the urban, 'British' protestant ideology of unionism.

This is a total falsification of reality. The rural, Gaelic model of Irishness, itself an artificial construct, means far less to a child of a catholic working class family from Dublin's inner city than it does to a protestant child from a rural background in the West of Ireland. I had personal experience of this when I discovered how baffled my friends from Dublin working class background were by their primary school Irish and English textbooks, with their stories like 'A Day on the Bog', which had a deep resonance for me. As a protestant I had less empathy with Jimín Máire Tadgh's religious vocation, but even then more of my neighbours probably entered catholic religious life than did the children of Ballyfermot or Finglas.

If that is true for the (catholic) working class of the south, how much more alien is this ideology to the catholic working class of Belfast and Derry? Although their religion is a badge of nationality, and in recent years learning Irish has become a mark of political consciousness, neither of these lead the people of the ghettoes to identify with the southern state.

This is less true of the northern catholic middle class, frequently rural in origin, whose advancement in the northern state was always blocked by discrimination. As the long association of the

Nationalist Party, and now the SDLP, with the main parties in the south attests, they could readily find a common identity with those who created, built and now sustain the southern state. Austin Currie found no difficulty in transplanting himself south and becoming a Fine Gael TD in Dublin.

The protestant population is not homogeneous either. In the south there are big cultural and political differences between people from urban and rural backgrounds, between the relatively poor members of the protestant churches who integrated with their catholic neighbours and those, richer, ones who did not. In the north too there are important social and cultural differences between protestants from different social and geographical backgrounds, though these are either latent or have been largely submerged by the recent developments of different degrees of unionism, outside of which they can find no expression,

The notion of 'two traditions' suits those who want to maintain the status quo of an Irish and crypto British state, fiddling only with superficialities. The reality is far more complex. Like all countries with a history of colonialism, 'tradition' in Ireland is composed of many strands, of successive waves of immigration, of a blending of traditions and the creation of new syntheses, of battles between classes and groups in which religion was forced into the background, of intermarriage and shared experiences between new and old immigrants.

No-one thinks this extraordinary when considering countries other than Ireland. Are the coloured and Indian populations of South Africa any less African than the black? Are the Spanish-derived or black people of Latin American countries any less Latin American than the native Indian peoples?

If we return to the rape image as appropriate to colonialism, the immigrants who came as colonisers inevitably bore the marks of their parentage. Yet no one would suggest making them pay for the sins of their father. That is, not unless they sought continued adherence to their rapacious parent and claimed special privileges because of his 'superiority', because of their whiter skin - or their religion. Yet the 'two traditions' idea implicitly endorses a pro-British tradition in Ireland as if it were a natural element, an act of nature, despite the fact that those who claimed Britishness also claim special privileges deriving from this status.

BEYOND NATIONALISM

The elements in Irish politics which feminists and socialists rightly identify as inimical to the interests of women and of workers are indeed to be found in the ideology built up around the twenty-six county state. But it is wrong to identify this with Irish nationalism, which has become deformed into twenty-six county pseudo-nationalism.

The search for the transformation of the conditions of the poor, many of them women, is not counterposed to the perspective of a totally free and independent Ireland in accordance with the liberationist message of revolutionary nationalism. On the contrary, the aspirations of workers, the poor and all the downtrodden and marginalised in Ireland can only ultimately be met in a framework other than that of the two states now in place on this island.

The only political tradition on this island which rejects the political institutions is that of the republican movement. However, because the republican movement does not seriously engage in any politics of a campaigning kind, postponing the resolution of all problems until the republican millenium, and has not explained its position in anything other than metaphysical terms, it fails to relate to the real concerns of the majority of the potentially disaffected and remains isolated. Nonetheless, at turning points in political life it has attracted considerable support because, I would argue, its rejection of the whole system struck an echo in the hearts and minds of those who sought a fundamental change in their circumstances.

Radical thinking in Ireland needs to reassess the heritage of the republican movement, whose concentration on the military campaign in the north and utter failure to respond to the social and economic problems of the population of the south, has obscured the potentially liberationist kernel of its message - that the political settlement of 1921 established a framework totally resistant to fundamental change, and that this settlement needs to be undone and a fresh start made.

This is not an argument for support for any wing of the republican movement as it exists today, but rather for the content of that tradition to be reintegrated into political debate, rather than excluded on the spurious basis that anyone engaging in that debate must first pass the litmus test of a McCarthyite declaration of the question of violence.

Apart from reassessing our own revolutionary heritage, which differs markedly from the political heritage of other European countries, we could learn from the other post-colonial societies which have also created political systems dedicated to preserving the essence of the social relations of the old society. The traditional parties of the left, while they exist, have singularly failed to challenge the established and governing parties in this country. But what has emerged more recently is a range of extra-parliamentary groups and movements, based on popular initiatives in local areas and specific campaigns on issues like the rights of minorities or in defence of the environment, which have generated widespread support and threaten the status quo. In Brazil (once one of the wealthiest countries in the world) this has led to the foundation of a new political party, the Workers Party, drawing all these movements together. In a few short years this party has succeeded in challenging, not only its rivals on the left, but the main representatives of the right.

So a sense of frustration with and alienation from political institutions need not be a cause for despair among people seeking change. On the contrary, it is to be welcomed as a basis for fresh and creative thinking and the organisation of the disaffected into movements and outlets not tied into these institutions. For almost seventy years the attempts to change Ireland through the political framework established out of the struggle for independence have failed and led people into false hopes. There are now multiple examples word-wide of alternatives to such a perspective.

Far from being ashamed of our colonial past, we should be happy to acknowledge and even embrace Ireland's status as a post-colonial society. Not only are fellow former colonies the centre of fresh thinking about politics in the world today, they are also the power-house of the most innovative art and culture, especially in the fields of literature and popular music. This is a far more exciting club to want to belong to than the complacent and paralysed world of the former colonialist, and present-day imperialist, powers.

In Europe, the countries of Eastern Europe are not as distant from our experience as we are led to believe. They too have similarities with our history (apart from the major difference of the second world war and its aftermath), they experienced a violation of democracy in the foundation and consolidation of their regimes, with a resulting question mark over their legitimacy which remained in the consciousness of the population. Intellectual activity tends to operate outside of, and in implicit opposition to, the established institutions. Nationalism, even though pushed into the background for decades, remains a powerful force in people's consciousness.

Then when eventually popular organisations break through the strait-jacket of repressive mechanisms and force conformism (as in Poland in 1981) they take totally new forms. *Solidarity* developed as much more than a trade union as this is traditionally understood, and more like an umbrella for a plethora of trade union, political, social and cultural movements, all more deeply rooted and more original than traditional parties or organisations. The resurgence of popular movements in East Germany and Czechoslovakia reveals people's capacity for political creativity outside of established institutions.

So a suspicion of illegitimacy is no bad thing for a state to have. The lack of faith in established institutions it engenders leaves great scope for the development of radical alternatives, movements which allow for people's self-expression in a way which established political parties and trade unions, dominated as they are by fossilised habits and entrenched bureaucracies, cannot do.

In the Irish context the fusion of such movements with a critique of the very basis of the southern state, and therefore of its twin in the north, could allow for the development of an alternative political vision which would go beyond the endless futile tinkering with the existing system and offer the hope of real emancipation to all the impoverished, disillusioned and marginalised in this country.

REFERENCES AND FURTHER READING

Andrews, AS. *Dublin Made Me* and *Man of No Property* Cork: Mercier Press, 1982

Boland, Kevin. *The Rise and Decline of Fianna Fáil* Cork: Mercier Press, 1982

Fanning, Ronan. 'The British Dimension in Ireland: Dependence and Independence' Dublin: *The Crane Bag* Vol 8 No 1, 1984

Ferns, HS. *The Argentine Republic* Newton Abbot: David and Charles / New York: Barnes & Noble, 1973

Galeano, Eduardo. *Open Veins of Latin America* New York: Monthly Review Press, 1973

Rupnik, Jacques. *The Other Europe* London: Weidenfeld & Nicholson, 1988

Said, Edward. *Yeats and Decolonisation* Derry: Field Day Pamphlet No 15, 1988

Ward, Margaret. *Unmanageable Revolutionaries* Dingle: Brandon Press / London: Pluto Press, 1983